ONE-POT VEGETARIAN

SABRINA FAUDA-RÔLE
PHOTOGRAPHY BY AKIKO IDA

Hardie Grant

BOOKS

CONTENTS

ONE-POT VEGETARIAN

PASTA OR OTHER
CARBOHYDRATES

VEGETABLE
PROTEINS

FRUIT OR
VEGETABLES

SPICES AND SEASONINGS

FATS OR CREAMY
INGREDIENTS

ALL IN ONE POT?

A one-pot vegetarian dish is a nutritionally complete vegetarian meal with everything cooked together in one pan. It's a quick and easy way to prepare a healthy balanced meal. Whether you opt for a traditional or original recipe, you can produce a perfect dish for an impromptu dinner party or a Sunday dinner.

The recipes in this book serve 2 to 8 people. Make sure you have a suitable hob to cook on, whether electric, gas or induction.

To make your shopping easy, all the ingredients can be found in a supermarket or wholefood shop. For a nutritionally complete one-pot vegetarian meal you will need a carbohydrate such as pasta, some plant-based protein, vegetables (in some cases combined with fruit), spices and a fat or creamy ingredient to give the dish depth and body.

7

Tips for a successful one-pot vegetarian dish:
- use fresh vegetables and choose your recipe according to the seasonal availability;
- gather together and weigh all the ingredients before you begin; wash and peel the vegetables;
- you can vary the recipes by changing the spices and seasonings or by serving with a garnish of snipped fresh herbs, crushed nuts, citrus zest, etc.

One-pot vegetarian dishes are often complete meals in one, but they can also be served with a green or raw vegetable salad. For non-vegetarians, they can be served as an accompaniment to fish or meat.

PUTTING TOGETHER A ONE-POT VEGETARIAN DISH

1.

CHOOSE YOUR GRAINS OR OTHER CARBOHYDRATES: pasta, rice, bulgur wheat, quinoa or potato, etc. Choose good-quality pasta that holds its shape when cooked. You can also use wholegrains or wholewheat pasta.

2.

USE FRESH OR FROZEN VEGETABLES for a well-balanced recipe. If you are using fresh vegetables, choose seasonal vegetables where possible, otherwise use frozen or dried. If you are using organic fresh vegetables, try not to peel them in order to to retain their vitamins.

3.

ADD VEGETABLE PROTEINS in the form of pulses (lentils, fresh, dried or tinned haricot (navy) beans, broad (fava) beans, chickpeas (garbanzos) etc.) or a soya-based ingredient such as tofu or tempeh.

4.

ADD A FAT OR CREAMY INGREDIENT to bind the various elements of the dish, give it a rich consistency and make a sauce. You can use dairy creams or plant-based creams made from soya, almonds, rice and coconut or butter, vegetable oils or cheese.

5.

INCLUDE AN INGREDIENT WITH A DISTINCTIVE FLAVOUR to add character to the dish, such as ginger, a smoked product, goat's cheese or dried mushrooms.

8

6.

ADD SPICES OR CONDIMENTS
to give your dish flavour and zing. You can use basic spices such as curry powder, paprika or cumin, but also lemon zest, ginger, lemongrass, soy sauce, miso, stock cubes or fresh, dried or frozen herbs, onions, shallots and garlic.

7.

USE COLD WATER:
use the quantities recommended in the recipes. Don't forget that a dish that contains a lot of fresh or frozen vegetables will release water while cooking.

8.

COOK FOR THE RECOMMENDED LENGTH OF TIME:
depending on the recipe, you may either need to stir while cooking or leave to cook without intervention.

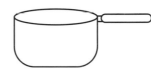

BASIC EQUIPMENT

FRYING PAN (SKILLET)

SAUCEPAN

WOODEN SPOON

KNIVES

CHOPPING BOARD

CASSEROLE DISH (DUTCH OVEN)

STORECUPBOARD BASICS

CARBOHYDRATES AND GRAINS

Good-quality pasta; rice: long-grain, short-grain, risotto, Nerone black, red Camargue, white or wholegrain rice; other grains: bulgur, pre-cooked wheat, semolina, spelt, barley, kasha (toasted buckwheat).

PRESERVED AND TINNED FOODS

Passata, tomato purée (paste), haricot (navy) beans, kidney beans, sweet corn, chickpeas (garbanzos), chestnuts, pesto, olives, sundried tomatoes.

CARTONS

Milk, unsweetened vegetable drinks, plant-based milks (soya, almond, spelt, rice, etc.), coconut milk.

VEGETABLE PROTEINS FOR A COMPLETE DISH

To produce a dish that is nutritionally complete even though it is vegetarian, you can include the vegetable proteins contained in the following foods:

- pulses (legumes) such as split peas, lentils, chickpeas (garbanzos) and mung beans;
- grains such as quinoa and spelt;
- nuts and seeds (cashews, macadamias, pecans, hazelnuts, almonds and sesame seeds);
- soya in all its forms: tofu, tempeh, miso.

PASTA, RICE, GRAINS AND PULSES

SMALL PASTA FOR SOUP
(SHOWN HERE: FUNGHINI)

RIGATONI

SPAGHETTI

FARFALLE

WHOLEWHEAT
SPAGHETTI

PRE-COOKED WHEAT
NOODLES

SMALL PASTA
SHELLS

12

BULGUR

WHEAT

SPLIT PEAS

RED
LENTILS

POLENTA

RED
CAMARGUE RICE

LONG-GRAIN
BASMATI RICE

FOR DEPTH AND FLAVOUR

COCONUT
OIL

GOAT'S
CHEESE

GORGONZOLA

SOYA-BASED
CREAM

PASSATA

HAZELNUT
DRINK

DOUBLE
(HEAVY) CREAM

14

CURRY
POWDER

LEMON
ZEST

THYME AND
BAY LEAVES

MISO PASTE

STOCK
CUBES

SMOKED
TOFU

FRESH
HERBS

GARLIC

15

ALL VEGETABLES

Recipes consisting entirely of vegetables – sautéed, simmered or stewed – to serve as a side or main dish, using an original and quick cooking method that gives a vitamin-rich result.

AUTUMN CASSEROLE

Preparation: 10 minutes
Cooking: 30 minutes

18

serves 6

350 g (12 oz) parsnips, cut into 1 cm (½ in) rounds
350 g (12 oz) sweet potatoes, peeled and cut into
    1 cm (½ in) rounds
100 g (3½ oz) carrots, peeled and cut into 1 cm
    (½ in) rounds
1 apple, peeled and quartered
1 onion, thinly sliced
1 cinnamon stick

50 g (2 oz) butter, cut into pieces
4 bay leaves
500 ml (17 fl oz/2 cups) water
2 pinches of salt
2 pinches of pepper

26 cm (10 in) casserole dish (Dutch oven)

method

Put all the ingredients into the casserole dish. Cover and simmer for
30 minutes over a medium heat.

VEGGIE HOTPOT

Preparation: 10 minutes
Cooking: 30 minutes

20

serves 6

500 g (1 lb 2 oz) green cabbage, thinly sliced
2 large carrots, peeled and thinly sliced
2 shallots, thinly sliced
1 garlic clove, chopped
50 g (2 oz/scant ½ cup) raisins
3 bay leaves
4 cloves
1 small bunch of dill, plus extra to serve

4 tablespoons olive oil
2 pinches of salt
2 pinches of pepper
500 ml (17 fl oz/2 cups) water
200 g (7 oz/generous ¾ cup) Greek yoghurt, to serve

26 cm (10 in) casserole dish (Dutch oven)

method

Put all the ingredients into the casserole dish, except for the water and yoghurt.
Sauté for 5 minutes over a high heat, stirring continuously. Add the water,
cover and simmer for 25 minutes over a low heat. Serve with the yoghurt
and reserved dill, snipped.

ROOT VEGETABLE CASSEROLE

Preparation: 10 minutes
Cooking: 20 minutes

serves 6

400 g (14 oz) multicoloured baby carrots
200 g (7 oz) Chioggia beetroots (beets), peeled and
  thinly sliced
200 g (7 oz) red beetroots (beets), peeled and
  thinly sliced
400 g (14 oz) parsnips, peeled and cut into 5 mm
  (¼ in) rounds
3 bay leaves
2 sprigs of thyme
200 ml (7 fl oz/scant 1 cup) water

1 teaspoon cumin seeds
1 tablespoon onion powder
1 garlic clove, chopped
2 pinches of salt
2 pinches of pepper
1 tablespoon honey
2 tablespoons olive oil
1 cinnamon stick

26 cm (10 in) casserole dish (Dutch oven)

method

Put all the vegetables into the casserole dish with the bay and thyme.
Pour in the water, sprinkle with cumin, then add the onion powder, garlic,
salt and pepper. Drizzle with honey and olive oil. Place the cinnamon stick
in the middle. Cover and cook for 20 minutes. Serve.

VEGETARIAN MAAFE

Preparation: 10 minutes
Cooking: 30 minutes

24

serves 6

800 g (1 lb 12 oz) pumpkin, peeled and cut into
  large cubes
2 carrots, peeled and cut into 1 cm (½ in) rounds
1 red (bell) pepper, cut into large squares
400 g (14 oz) potatoes, cut into large cubes
1 small green chilli, chopped
1 tablespoon tomato purée (paste)
200 g (7 oz/generous ¾ cup) peanut butter

750 ml (25 fl oz/3 cups) water
1 vegetable stock cube
2 pinches of salt
2 pinches of pepper
50 g (2 oz/⅓ cup) peanuts, toasted, salted and
  roughly chopped, to serve (optional)

26 cm (10 in) casserole dish (Dutch oven)

method

Put all the ingredients into the casserole dish, setting aside half the chopped chilli. Simmer for 30 minutes over a medium heat, stirring occasionally. Add the reserved chilli, to garnish. If liked, sprinkle with the chopped toasted peanuts, to serve.

FENNEL AND ORANGE CASSEROLE

Preparation: 5 minutes
Cooking: 25 minutes

26

serves 4

2 large fennel bulbs, halved and then sliced
  (set aside the green leaves)
1 orange, thinly sliced
½ lemon, quartered
2 tablespoons honey
1 cinnamon stick
1 teaspoon fennel seeds

3 tablespoons olive oil
1 tablespoon onion powder
2 pinches of salt
2 pinches of pepper

30 cm (12 in) frying pan (skillet)

method

Put all the ingredients into the frying pan, except for the fennel
leaves. Sauté for 3 minutes over a high heat, stirring continuously.
Lower the heat, cover, and cook for 20 minutes, stirring regularly.
Serve with the reserved fennel leaves, snipped.

BRUSSELS SPROUT CASSEROLE
WITH CHESTNUTS

Preparation: 5 minutes
Cooking: 15 minutes

serves 6

600 g (1 lb 5 oz) frozen Brussels sprouts
200 g (7 oz) tinned chestnuts
2 tablespoons wholegrain mustard
200 ml (7 fl oz/scant 1 cup) double (heavy) cream
1 onion, thinly sliced

1 pinch of nutmeg
2 sprigs of rosemary
500 ml (17 fl oz/2 cups) water

26 cm (10 in) casserole dish (Dutch oven)

method

Put all the ingredients into the casserole dish. Bring to the boil then simmer,
covered, for 15 minutes over a medium heat. Serve.

WINTER CASSEROLE

Preparation: 10 minutes
Cooking: 20 minutes

serves 6

600 g (1 lb 5 oz) frozen salsify
400 g (14 oz) florets of Romanesco
1 small purple turnip, quartered
1 small golden ball turnip, quartered
100 g (3½ oz) butter
1 pinch of saffron

300 ml (10 fl oz/1¼ cups) water
3 pinches of salt
2 pinches of pepper

26 cm (10 in) casserole dish (Dutch oven)

method

Put all the ingredients into the casserole dish. Cover and simmer for
20 minutes over a medium heat. Serve.

FRENCH-STYLE PEAS

Preparation: 5 minutes
Cooking: 15 minutes

32

serves 6

600 g (1 lb 5 oz) frozen peas
6 lettuce leaves
1 carrot, peeled and cut into 1 cm (½ in) rounds
3 spring onions (scallions), halved lengthways
50 g (2 oz) salted butter
1 vegetable stock cube
200 ml (7 fl oz) water
2 pinches of pepper

20 cm (8 in) saucepan

method

Put all the ingredients into the saucepan. Bring to the boil and simmer, covered, for 15 minutes over a medium heat. Serve.

SPRING GREEN CASSEROLE

Preparation: 10 minutes
Cooking: 15 minutes

serves 6

150 g (5 oz) green beans, topped and tailed
250 g (9 oz) mangetout
100 g (3½ oz) baby spinach
200 g (7 oz) courgettes (zucchini), cut into rounds
50 g (2 oz) butter, cut into pieces
1 sprig of basil

200 ml (7 fl oz/scant 1 cup) water
2 pinches of salt
2 pinches of pepper

26 cm (10 in) casserole dish (Dutch oven)

34

method

Put all the ingredients into the casserole dish. Cover and simmer for
15 minutes over a medium heat. Serve.

CAPONATA

Preparation: 15 minutes
Cooking: 1 hour

36

serves 6

6 tablespoons olive oil
4 large aubergines (eggplants), diced
6 garlic cloves, chopped
1 courgette (zucchini), diced
2 red (bell) peppers, diced
2 large stalks of celery with leaves, thinly sliced
200 g (7 oz/generous ¾ cup) tomato purée (paste)

200 g (7 oz/1⅔ cups) green olives, pitted
150 g (5 oz) capers, drained
100 ml (3½ fl oz/scant ½ cup) balsamic vinegar
50 g (2 oz/¼ cup) sugar

26 cm (10 in) casserole dish (Dutch oven)

method

Heat the oil in the casserole dish over a medium heat. Sauté the aubergines and garlic for 15 minutes, stirring. Add the courgette, cook for 5 minutes, then add the peppers and celery. Cook for a further 5 minutes, stirring. Add the tomato purée, olives, capers, vinegar and sugar. Stir well and cook, covered, for 35 minutes over a low heat, stirring regularly. Serve hot or cold.

PAN-FRIED CARROTS AND POTATOES

Preparation: 10 minutes
Cooking: 35 minutes

38

serves 4

750 g (1 lb 10 oz) potatoes, peeled and diced
500 g (1 lb 2 oz) carrots, peeled and cut into
   1 cm (½ in) rounds
2 onions, thinly sliced
3 garlic cloves, unpeeled
3 sprigs of rosemary

4 tablespoons olive oil
4 eggs (optional)
salt and pepper, to season

30 cm (12 in) frying pan (skillet)

method

Put all the ingredients into the frying pan except for the eggs. Sauté for 30 minutes over a medium heat, stirring very regularly. If using, crack the eggs into the pan. Cover and cook for a further 4 minutes. Season with salt and pepper before serving.

FRIED PLANTAINS

Preparation: 10 minutes
Cooking: 15 minutes

40

serves 4

8 tablespoons coconut oil
2 large very ripe plantains, peeled and cut
   into 1 cm (½ in) rounds
2 large parsnips, peeled and cut into
   1 cm (½ in) rounds

2 spring onions (scallions), thinly sliced
1 teaspoon turmeric
salt and pepper, to season

30 cm (12 in) frying pan (skillet)

method

Heat the oil in the frying pan over a medium heat and fry the plantain
and parsnip rounds for 5 minutes. Turn over the rounds, sprinkle with
the thinly sliced onions and turmeric and cook for a further 5 minutes.
Stir and cook for 3 minutes. Season with salt and pepper and serve.

JERUSALEM ARTICHOKE AND GOAT'S CHEESE MASH

Preparation: 10 minutes
Cooking: 30 minutes

42

serves 4

750 g (1 lb 10 oz) Jerusalem artichokes,
    peeled and halved
750 g (1 lb 10 oz) small mashing potatoes,
    peeled and halved
3 tablespoons olive oil
2 sprigs of rosemary, plus extra to serve

500 ml (17 fl oz/2 cups) water
200 g (7 oz) goat's cheese
salt and pepper, to season

26 cm (10 in) casserole dish (Dutch oven)

method

Put all the ingredients into the casserole dish, except for the goat's cheese. Cover and cook for 30 minutes over a medium heat until the potatoes become very soft. Remove the rosemary and crush the mixture with a fork as you add the goat's cheese. Season with salt and pepper and serve with the reserved rosemary.

HARICOT BEAN PURÉE WITH PAPRIKA

Preparation: 5 minutes
Cooking: 35 minutes

44

serves 6

600 g (1 lb 5 oz) frozen haricot (navy) beans
1 small (100 g/3½ oz) courgette (zucchini),
   cut into rounds
1 small onion, thinly sliced
2 garlic cloves
200 ml (7 fl oz/scant 1 cup) double (heavy) cream
1 vegetable stock cube
1 tablespoon paprika, plus extra to serve

1 tablespoon tomato purée (paste)
2 tablespoons olive oil
2 tablespoons sherry vinegar
2 pinches of salt
2 pinches of pepper
1 litre (34 fl oz/4 cups) water

26 cm (10 in) casserole dish (Dutch oven)

method

Put all the ingredients into the casserole dish, setting aside half the cream for serving. Bring to the boil and then cook for 30 minutes over a medium heat, stirring regularly. Blend, then serve with a spoonful of cream and a sprinkle of paprika.

STIR-FRIED KALE, PECAN AND LEMON

Preparation: 10 minutes
Cooking: 10 minutes

serves 4

500 g (1 lb 2 oz) kale
50 g (2 oz/½ cup) pecan nuts
2 tablespoons sugar
2 tablespoons olive oil
3 tablespoons soy sauce

20 g (¾ oz) ginger, chopped
zest of 1 lemon

30 cm (12 in) casserole dish (Dutch oven)

method

Rinse the kale and tear off the central stalk. Heat the nuts and sugar in the
casserole dish for 5 minutes over a high heat, stirring until caramelised,
then take out the nuts. Leave to cool, then roughly chop. Add the olive oil,
then the kale. Sauté for 5 minutes, then add the soy sauce and ginger.
Mix well and serve with the lemon zest and the chopped nuts.

RED CABBAGE AND BLACK BEAN STEW

Preparation: 10 minutes
Cooking: 20 minutes

serves 4

20 g (¾ oz) butter
500 g (1 lb 2 oz) red cabbage, thinly sliced
50 g (2 oz/¼ cup) sugar
1 onion, thinly sliced
1 pinch of nutmeg
2 tablespoons dried oregano

2 pinches of salt
350 g (12 oz) tinned black beans, drained
150 ml (5 fl oz/scant ⅔ cup) water

26 cm (10 in) casserole dish (Dutch oven)

method

Melt the butter in the casserole dish, then add all the ingredients except for the beans and water. Cover and cook for 15 minutes over a medium heat, stirring regularly. Add the beans and water. Stir and cook for a further 5 minutes before serving.

PLANT-BASED PROTEINS

Traditional recipes revisited in vegetarian form,
as well as original combinations for discovering
or rediscovering grains, pulses (legumes) and tofu.

CREAMY LENTILS WITH SPINACH

Preparation: 10 minutes
Cooking: 30 minutes

serves 6

250 g (9 oz) green lentils
400 g (14 oz) potatoes, cut into large cubes
1 onion, thinly sliced
1 carrot, peeled and cut into 2 cm (¾ in) rounds
1 sprig of thyme
2 bay leaves
600 g (1 lb 5 oz) frozen spinach

300 ml (10 fl oz/1¼ cups) single (light) cream
250 ml (8½ fl oz/1 cup) white wine
1 garlic clove
2 pinches of salt
2 pinches of pepper

26 cm (10 in) casserole dish (Dutch oven)

method

Put all the ingredients into the casserole dish and simmer for 30 minutes over a medium heat, stirring regularly. Remove the garlic clove before serving.

LENTILS, QUINOA AND PEPPERS

Preparation: 5 minutes
Cooking: 25 minutes

54

serves 4

150 g (5 oz/¾ cup) beluga lentils
150 g (5 oz/¾ cup) quinoa
2 (bell) peppers (red and yellow), thinly sliced
1 onion, thinly sliced
1 garlic clove, chopped
3 sprigs of parsley, snipped, plus extra to serve

2 tablespoons soy sauce, plus extra to serve
2 tablespoons olive oil
750 ml (25 fl oz/3 cups) water
2 pinches of salt

26 cm (10 in) casserole dish (Dutch oven)

55

method

Put all the ingredients into the casserole dish. Simmer for 25 minutes over
a medium heat, stirring regularly. Serve with the reserved fresh
parsley and soy sauce.

DAHL

Preparation: 10 minutes
Cooking: 30 minutes

56

serves 6

250 g (9 oz/1 cup) red lentils
400 g (14 oz) butternut squash, peeled, deseeded
   and cut into cubes
2 tablespoons tomato purée (paste)
1 onion, thinly sliced
1 garlic clove, chopped
200 ml (7 fl oz/scant 1 cup) single (light) cream
1 pinch of chilli powder

1 teaspoon curry powder
4 cardamom pods, crushed
1 litre (34 fl oz/4 cups) water
2 pinches of salt
2 pinches of pepper
1 small sprig of coriander (cilantro)

30 cm (12 in) frying pan (skillet)

method

Put all the ingredients into the frying pan, setting aside half the coriander. Cook for 30 minutes over a low heat, stirring regularly. Serve with the reserved coriander.

VEGGIE COUSCOUS

Preparation: 15 minutes
Cooking: 35 minutes

58

serves 4

2 tablespoons olive oil
1 onion, thinly sliced
3 tablespoons ras el-hanout
400 g (14 oz) turnips, peeled and quartered
6 carrots, cut into 3 cm (1 in) rounds
500 g (1 lb 2 oz) potimarron (red kuri) squash,
   deseeded and sliced
70 g (2¼ oz) tomato purée (paste)
1 teaspoon harissa, plus extra to serve

2 tablespoons raisins
2 stock cubes
2 pinches of salt
1 litre (34 fl oz/4 cups) water
4 courgettes (zucchini), cut into 2 cm (¾ in) rounds
400 g (14 oz) tinned chickpeas
300 g (10½ oz/1⅔ cups) couscous

26 cm (10 in) casserole dish (Dutch oven)

method

Heat the oil in the casserole dish and sauté the onion with the ras el-hanout. Add the turnips, carrots, potimarron squash, tomato purée, harissa, raisins, stock cubes and salt. Cover with water and simmer for 20 minutes over a medium heat. Add the courgettes and chickpeas and simmer for 10 minutes, stirring. Put 75 g (2½ oz) couscous into each of 4 bowls and pour over 1 ladle of cooking stock. Cover and leave for 5 minutes to swell. Serve with the vegetables and reserved harissa.

SHAKSHUKA

Preparation: 10 minutes
Cooking: 20 minutes

60

serves 4

1 onion, thinly sliced
3 (bell) peppers (multicoloured), thinly sliced
1 teaspoon cumin seeds
1 pinch of saffron
4 tablespoons olive oil
400 g (14 oz) tinned whole tomatoes
2 pinches of salt

1 pinch of pepper
4 eggs
1 small sprig of coriander (cilantro), snipped, to serve
1 small green chilli, chopped, to serve

30 cm (12 in) frying pan (skillet)

method

Sauté the onion, peppers, cumin and saffron in the oil for 5 minutes. Add the tinned tomatoes, salt and pepper and mix well, crushing the tomatoes. Cover and cook for 10 minutes, stirring regularly. Break the eggs into the mixture, and cook for a further 3 minutes. Serve with the coriander and chilli.

BULGUR AND CAULIFLOWER CURRY

Preparation: 10 minutes
Cooking: 20 minutes
Resting: 10 minutes

serves 4

350 g (12 oz/2 cups) coarse bulgur wheat
350 g (12 oz) grated cauliflower
20 g (¾ oz) chia seeds
300 ml (10 fl oz/1¼ cups) single (light) cream
1 teaspoon curry powder
50 g (2 oz/scant ½ cup) raisins

1 teaspoon coriander seeds, crushed
500 ml (17 fl oz/2 cups) water
1 teaspoon salt
1 pinch of pepper

30 cm (12 in) casserole dish (Dutch oven)

method

Put all the ingredients into the casserole dish and cook for 20 minutes over a medium heat, stirring occasionally. Remove from the heat and leave to rest, covered, for 10 minutes before serving.

EINKORN, APPLE AND GOAT'S CHEESE RISOTTO

Preparation: 10 minutes
Cooking: 1 hour

64

serves 6

250 g (9 oz) einkorn
2 small apples, grated
1 onion, thinly sliced
150 g (5 oz) small button mushrooms
150 g (7 oz) goat's cheese, plus 50 g (2 oz) to serve
1 teaspoon coriander seeds
2 sprigs of rosemary, plus extra to serve

2 tablespoons olive oil
1 litre (34 fl oz/4 cups) water
2 pinches of salt
2 pinches of pepper

26 cm (10 in) casserole dish (Dutch oven)

method

Put all the ingredients into the casserole dish. Cook for 1 hour over a low heat, stirring regularly until all the water has evaporated. Serve with the reserved sprigs of rosemary and small pieces of goat's cheese.

TAGINE

Preparation: 10 minutes
Cooking: 45 minutes

serves 4

400 g (14 oz) frozen artichoke bottoms
300 g (10½ oz) frozen peeled broad (fava) beans
350 g (12 oz) butternut squash, deseeded and cut
   into large chunks
150 g (5 oz/¾ cup) pearl barley
2 preserved lemons, quartered
1 onion, thinly sliced
50 g (2 oz/⅓ cup) whole almonds
50 g (2 oz/½ cup) green olives, pitted

2 sticks of cinnamon
1 tablespoon ras el-hanout
1 tablespoon honey
1 litre (34 fl oz/4 cups) water
1 tablespoon salt
2 pinches of pepper

26 cm (10 in) casserole dish (Dutch oven)

method

Put all the ingredients into the casserole dish. Simmer for 45 minutes
over a low heat. Serve.

AUBERGINES AND TOASTED BUCKWHEAT

Preparation: 10 minutes
Cooking: 35 minutes

serves 4

4 tablespoons olive oil
500 g (1 lb 2 oz) aubergines (eggplants), diced
250 g (9 oz) toasted buckwheat (kasha)
500 ml (17 fl oz/2 cups) water
1 teaspoon salt

2 tablespoons honey
2 sprigs of mint, snipped, to serve
2 tablespoons golden sesame seeds, to serve

30 cm (12 in) casserole dish (Dutch oven)

method

Heat the oil in the casserole dish. Sauté the aubergines for 15 minutes.
Add the buckwheat and sauté for a further 5 minutes. Add the water and
salt. Cook for 10 minutes, until the water has completely evaporated.
Stir in the honey and caramelise for 5 minutes. Serve with the
snipped mint and sesame seeds.

SWEET POTATO AND WHITE BEAN STEW

Preparation: 10 minutes
Cooking: 30 minutes

70

serves 4

800 g (1 lb 12 oz) sweet potatoes, peeled and diced
1 onion, thinly sliced
800 g (1 lb 12 oz) tinned haricot (navy) beans, drained
400 g (14 oz/1⅔ cups) passata (sieved tomatoes)
1 garlic clove, chopped
1 teaspoon paprika
1 teaspoon cinnamon
1 pinch of ground nutmeg

1 pinch of hot chilli powder
2 tablespoons olive oil
250 ml (8½ fl oz/1 cup) water
1 pinch of salt
1 pinch of pepper
1 small sprig of coriander (cilantro)

26 cm (10 in) casserole dish (Dutch oven)

method

Put all the ingredients into the casserole dish, setting aside half the coriander.
Cover and cook for approximately 30 minutes over a medium heat.
Serve with the reserved coriander, snipped.

POLENTA AND MUSHROOM CAKE

Preparation: 5 minutes
Cooking: 8 minutes

72

serves 4

150 g (5 oz/1 cup) polenta
200 g (7 oz) button mushrooms, quartered
50 g (2 oz/⅓ cup) sundried tomatoes, chopped
2 tablespoons onion powder
2 sprigs of thyme, destalked
30 g (1 oz) butter, cut into pieces

1 pinch of salt
1 pinch of pepper
500 ml (17 fl oz/2 cups) milk
2 tablespoons grated Parmesan, plus extra to serve

30 cm (12 in) frying pan (skillet)

method

Put all the ingredients, except the milk and Parmesan, into the frying pan. Cook for 3 minutes over a low heat, stirring to melt the butter. Add the milk and Parmesan. Bring to the boil and cook for 5 minutes, stirring so that the polenta thickens. Serve hot or cool, with the reserved Parmesan.

QUINOA AND SWEET POTATO CURRY

Preparation: 5 minutes
Cooking: 25 minutes
Resting: 15 minutes

serves 4

350 g (12 oz/1¾ cups) quinoa
500 g (1 lb 2 oz) sweet potato, peeled and diced
400 ml (13 fl oz) tin coconut milk
2 tablespoons curry powder
1 onion, thinly sliced
1 garlic clove, chopped

400 ml (13 fl oz/generous 1½ cups) water
2 pinches of salt
1 pinch of pepper

26 cm (10 in) casserole dish (Dutch oven)

method

Put all the ingredients into the casserole dish. Simmer for 25 minutes over a medium heat, stirring regularly. Remove from the heat and leave to rest for 15 minutes before serving.

SPLIT PEA AND SMOKED TOFU STEW

Soaking: 1 hour
Preparation: 10 minutes
Cooking: 40 minutes

serves 4

300 g (10½ oz/1⅓ cups) split peas
4 carrots, peeled and diced
1 onion, thinly sliced
1 garlic clove
1 vegetable stock cube
100 g (3½ oz) smoked tofu, diced

1 sprig of thyme
1.5 litres (51 fl oz/6 cups) water
2 pinches of salt
1 small bunch of parsley

20 cm (8 in) saucepan

method

Soak the split peas in cold water for 1 hour. Rinse. Put all the ingredients into the saucepan, setting aside half the parsley. Cook for 40 minutes over a low heat, stirring well. Serve with the reserved fresh parsley, snipped.

TOFU AND MUSHROOM STEW

Preparation: 10 minutes
Cooking: 20 minutes

serves 4

750 g (1 lb 10 oz) mixed fresh mushrooms
250 g (9 oz) smoked tofu with herbs, diced
2 bay leaves
2 sprigs of thyme
250 ml (8½ fl oz/1 cup) soya-based cream

4 sprigs of parsley, snipped, plus extra to serve
2 pinches of salt
2 pinches of pepper

26 cm (10 in) casserole dish (Dutch oven)

method

Put all the ingredients into the casserole dish and simmer for 20 minutes over a medium heat, stirring regularly. Serve with the reserved parsley.

SAUTÉED TOFU AND SPINACH MASALA

Preparation: 10 minutes
Cooking: 15 minutes
Resting: 5 minutes

serves 4

2 tablespoons olive oil
1 spring onion (scallion), thinly sliced
20 g (¾ oz) ginger, peeled and chopped
500 g (1 lb 2 oz) plain tofu, diced
2 tablespoons garam masala

4 tablespoons soy sauce
150 g (5 oz) baby spinach
50 g (2 oz/⅓ cup) cashew nuts, chopped, to serve

30 cm (12 in) casserole dish (Dutch oven)

method

Heat the oil in the casserole dish and sauté the onion and ginger for
5 minutes. Add the tofu and garam masala and sauté for 5 minutes.
Add the soy sauce and cook for 5 minutes. Turn off the heat and
then add the spinach. Cover and leave to rest for 5 minutes.
Stir and serve with the cashew nuts.

SAUTÉED TOFU, BROCCOLI AND BUTTERNUT SQUASH

Preparation: 10 minutes
Cooking: 15 minutes

serves 4

4 tablespoons olive oil
500 g (1 lb 2 oz) butternut squash, peeled and grated
20 g (¾ oz) ginger, peeled and chopped
250 g (9 oz) herb tofu, diced
florets from 1 small head of broccoli, sliced

4 tablespoons soy sauce
2 tablespoons grated coconut, to serve

30 cm (12 in) casserole dish (Dutch oven)

method

Heat the oil in the casserole dish. Sauté the butternut squash, ginger,
tofu and broccoli for 10 minutes. Add the soy sauce and cook
for a further 5 minutes. Serve sprinkled with coconut.

STIR-FRIED SWEET POTATOES AND TEMPEH

Preparation: 10 minutes
Cooking: 25 minutes

84

serves 4

2 tablespoons olive oil
1 kg (2 lb 4 oz) sweet potatoes, peeled and diced
200 g (7 oz) tempeh, diced
2 shallots, thinly sliced
4 tablespoons maple syrup

4 tablespoons soy sauce
4 sprigs of coriander (cilantro)
1 tablespoon toasted sesame seeds

30 cm (12 in) casserole dish (Dutch oven)

method

Heat the oil in the casserole dish and sauté the sweet potatoes, tempeh and shallots for 15 minutes. Add the maple syrup and stir regularly until the mixture caramelises. Add the soy sauce and stir for a further 5 minutes until you have a syrupy sauce. Serve sprinkled with the fresh coriander, snipped, and sesame seeds.

TUSCAN SOUP

Preparation: 10 minutes
Cooking: 50 minutes

serves 4

1 fennel bulb, finely diced
2 carrots, peeled and thinly sliced
6 stalks of celery, chopped, plus a few leaves to serve
250 g (9 oz) smoked tofu, diced
1 onion, thinly sliced
2 sprigs of rosemary
2 garlic cloves, chopped
1 pinch of chilli powder

1 tablespoon aniseed
4 tablespoons olive oil
400 g (14 oz) tinned whole tomatoes
1.5 litres (51 fl oz/6 cups) water
1 teaspoon salt
200 g (7 oz) dry bread, cubed, to serve

26 cm (10 in) casserole dish (Dutch oven)

method

Put all the ingredients into the casserole dish except for the tomatoes, water and salt. Cook for 5 minutes over a high heat, stirring. Add the tomatoes, water and salt. Cook for 45 minutes over a low heat. Serve with the cubes of bread and reserved celery leaves, snipped.

VEGETARIAN POT-AU-FEU

Preparation: 10 minutes
Cooking: 30 minutes

serves 6

500 g (1 lb 2 oz) green cabbage, quartered
3 carrots, halved
3 turnips, halved
2 leeks, cut into thirds
1 onion, halved
1 small bunch of parsley
2 bay leaves
2 garlic cloves

2 sprigs of thyme
2 tablespoons miso
3 cloves
2 litres (70 fl oz/8 cups) water
1 teaspoon salt
2 pinches of pepper

26 cm (10 in) casserole dish (Dutch oven)

method

Put all the ingredients into the casserole dish. Cover and simmer
for 30 minutes over a medium heat.

SAVOURY PORRIDGE

Preparation: 5 minutes
Cooking: 5 minutes
Resting: 5 minutes

serves 4

50 g (2 oz/½ cup) rolled oats
500 ml (17 fl oz/2 cups) milk, of any variety
100 g (3½ oz) button mushrooms, thinly sliced
2 sprigs of thyme
20 g (¾ oz) chia seeds
100 g (3½ oz/¾ cup) frozen peas
2 tablespoons tamari

1 pinch of grated nutmeg
1 pinch of pepper
2 tablespoons sesame seeds
1 avocado, to serve

20 cm (8 in) saucepan

method

Put all the ingredients into the saucepan, setting aside half the sesame seeds.
Bring to the boil and cook for 3 minutes over a medium heat, stirring.
Cover and allow to rest for 5 minutes. Serve with slices of
avocado and sprinkled with the reserved sesame seeds.

TOMATO AND SWEETCORN POLENTA CAKE

Preparation: 5 minutes
Cooking: 11 minutes

serves 4

3 tablespoons olive oil
1 spring onion (scallion), thinly sliced
350 g (12 oz) tinned sweetcorn, drained
500 g (1 lb 2 oz) cherry tomatoes
150 g (5 oz/1 cup) polenta
2 pinches of salt

1 pinch of pepper
500 ml (17 fl oz/2 cups) water
grated Cheddar, to serve

30 cm (12 in) frying pan (skillet)

method

Heat the oil in the frying pan. Sauté the spring onion with the sweetcorn and tomatoes for 5 minutes. Add the polenta, salt and pepper. Stir well and add the water. Cook for 1 minute, stirring, then cook for 5 minutes over a low heat to allow the polenta to thicken. Serve with grated Cheddar.

PASTA, RICE AND GNOCCHI

Cook in a small amount of water for perfect results
and maximum flavour. Here are several traditional
recipes and some more original combinations
for a new take on rice and pasta dishes.

SPAGHETTI WITH TOMATOES AND BASIL

Preparation: 10 minutes
Cooking: 15 minutes

96

serves 4

350 g (12 oz) spaghetti
2 garlic cloves, thinly sliced
1 onion, thinly sliced
400 g (14 oz) cherry tomatoes, halved
4 tablespoons olive oil
1 pinch of chilli powder
2 tablespoons tomato purée (paste)

20 basil leaves, plus extra to serve
1 litre (34 fl oz/4 cups) water
1 tablespoon salt
2 pinches of pepper
grated Parmesan, to serve

26 cm (10 in) casserole dish (Dutch oven)

method

Put all the ingredients into the casserole dish and cook for approximately 15 minutes over a medium heat, stirring regularly. Serve with the reserved fresh basil leaves and Parmesan.

LINGUINE WITH COURGETTE AND LEMON

Preparation: 5 minutes
Cooking: 15 minutes

98

serves 4

350 g (12 oz) linguine
1 large courgette (zucchini), cut into strips with a
    vegetable peeler
200 ml (7 fl oz/scant 1 cup) double (heavy) cream
zest of 1 lemon
1 small bunch of dill, snipped, plus extra to serve
1 vegetable stock cube
1 litre (34 fl oz/4 cups) water

20 cm (8 in) saucepan

method

Put all the ingredients into the saucepan and cook for approximately 15 minutes over a medium heat, stirring regularly. Serve with the reserved dill, snipped.

FARFALLE WITH BLUE CHEESE AND MUSHROOMS

Preparation: 10 minutes
Cooking: 15 minutes

serves 4

350 g (12 oz) farfalle
250 g (9 oz) mixed mushrooms, thinly sliced
1 onion, thinly sliced
150 g (5 oz) blue cheese, such as Fourme d'Ambert
200 ml (7 fl oz/scant 1 cup) spelt-based or
   other cream
1 teaspoon coriander seeds

2 tablespoons olive oil
1 teaspoon salt
2 pinches of pepper
1 litre (34 fl oz/4 cups) water

26 cm (10 in) casserole dish (Dutch oven)

method

Put all the ingredients into the casserole dish and cook for approximately
15 minutes over a medium heat, stirring regularly. Serve.

VEGGIE SPAG BOL

Preparation: 10 minutes
Cooking: 15 minutes

102

serves 4

350 g (12 oz) spaghetti
1 onion, thinly sliced
350 g (12 oz/1⅓ cups) passata (sieved tomatoes)
1 carrot, peeled and thinly sliced
2 sprigs of thyme
2 bay leaves
150 g (5 oz) tempeh, chopped
1 garlic clove, chopped
1 litre (34 fl oz/4 cups) water

2 pinches of salt
2 pinches of pepper
grated Parmesan, to serve

26 cm (10 in) casserole dish (Dutch oven)

method

Put all the ingredients into the casserole dish and cook for approximately 15 minutes over a medium heat, stirring regularly. Serve with grated Parmesan.

ORECCHIETTE WITH AUBERGINE AND MOZZARELLA

Preparation: 10 minutes
Cooking: 15 minutes

104

serves 4

350 g (12 oz) orecchiette
2 garlic cloves, chopped
150 g (5 oz) frozen grilled sliced aubergines (eggplants)
200 g (7 oz/scant 1 cup) passata (sieved tomatoes)
1 small onion, thinly sliced
1 small bunch of parsley, snipped, plus extra to serve

1 tablespoon dried oregano
2 tablespoons olive oil
1.2 litres (40 fl oz/4¾ cups) water
150 g (5 oz) balls of mozzarella, to serve

26 cm (10 in) casserole dish (Dutch oven)

method

Put all the ingredients into the casserole dish except for the mozzarella.
Cook for approximately 15 minutes over a medium heat, stirring
regularly. Mix with the mozzarella balls and serve with the reserved
fresh parsley, snipped.

PENNE WITH PEPPERS AND MASCARPONE

Preparation: 5 minutes
Cooking: 15 minutes

serves 4

350 g (12 oz) penne
3 multicoloured (bell) peppers, thinly sliced
250 g (9 oz) mascarpone
100 g (3½ oz/scant 1 cup) black olives
1 tablespoon dried oregano
2 tablespoons olive oil

1 litre (34 fl oz/4 cups) water
2 pinches of salt
2 pinches of pepper

26 cm (10 in) casserole dish (Dutch oven)

method

Put all the ingredients into the casserole dish and cook for approximately
15 minutes over a medium heat, stirring regularly. Serve.

SPAGHETTI WITH BROCCOLI AND ALMONDS

Preparation: 10 minutes
Cooking: 15 minutes

108

serves 4

350 g (12 oz) wholewheat spaghetti
500 g (1 lb 2 oz) broccoli florets
1 onion, thinly sliced
200 ml (7 fl oz/scant 1 cup) almond cream
2 sprigs of thyme
2 tablespoons toasted flaked almonds, plus extra to serve
2 tablespoons soy sauce, plus extra to serve

2 pinches of salt
2 pinches of pepper
1 litre (34 fl oz/4 cups) water
grated Parmesan, to serve

26 cm (10 in) casserole dish (Dutch oven)

method

Put all the ingredients into the casserole dish and cook for approximately
15 minutes over a medium heat, stirring regularly. Serve with a few toasted
flaked almonds, the reserved soy sauce and the grated Parmesan.

RIGATONI WITH TOMATO AND CHICKPEAS

Preparation: 5 minutes
Cooking: 15 minutes

110

serves 4

350 g (12 oz) rigatoni
350 g (12 oz) tinned chickpeas (garbanzos), drained
400 g (14 oz) tinned chopped tomatoes
50 g (2 oz/½ cup) green olives, pitted
1 tablespoon dried oregano
1 pinch of chilli powder
2 tablespoons olive oil

1 onion, thinly sliced
800 ml (27 fl oz/3¼ cups) water
2 pinches of salt
2 pinches of pepper
grated Emmental, to serve

26 cm (10 in) casserole dish (Dutch oven)

method

Put all the ingredients into the dish and cook for approximately 15 minutes over a medium heat, stirring regularly. Serve with the grated Emmental.

MAC AND CHEESE

Preparation: 5 minutes
Cooking: 15 minutes
Resting: 10 minutes

serves 4

350 g (12 oz) elbow macaroni
400 ml (13 fl oz) tin unsweetened evaporated milk
1 teaspoon wholegrain mustard
1 tablespoon smoked paprika
100 g (3½ oz) Cheddar, diced
1 tablespoon onion powder
1 garlic clove, chopped

800 ml (27 fl oz/3¼ cups) water
2 pinches of salt
2 pinches of pepper
100 g (3½ oz/1 cup) grated Parmesan
100 g (3½ oz/1 cup) grated Emmental

30 cm (12 in) frying pan (skillet)

method

Put all the ingredients into the frying pan, except for the Parmesan
and Emmental. Cook for 15 minutes over a medium heat, stirring very
regularly. Cover and leave to rest for 10 minutes. Stir in the Parmesan
and Emmental before serving.

TOMATO TORTELLINI

Preparation: 5 minutes
Cooking: 10 minutes

serves 4

300 g (10½ oz) spinach tortellini
200 g (7 oz/scant 1 cup) passata (sieved tomatoes)
1 carrot, grated
1 spring onion (scallion), thinly sliced
2 sprigs of basil, snipped, plus extra to serve
2 tablespoons olive oil

250 ml (8½ fl oz/1 cup) water
1 pinch of salt
2 pinches of pepper
250 g (9 oz) ricotta

30 cm (12 in) frying pan (skillet)

method

Put all the ingredients into the frying pan, setting aside half the ricotta.
Cook for 10 minutes over a medium heat. Serve with the reserved fresh
basil and ricotta.

TAGLIATELLE WITH GORGONZOLA AND WALNUTS

Preparation: 5 minutes
Cooking: 15 minutes

116

serves 4

350 g (12 oz) fresh tagliatelle
3 courgettes (zucchini), grated
200 g (7 oz) Gorgonzola
100 g (3½ oz/1 cup) walnuts
750 ml (25 fl oz/3 cups) water

2 pinches of salt
2 pinches of pepper

30 cm (12 in) casserole dish (Dutch oven)

method

Put all the ingredients into the casserole dish and cook for approximately
15 minutes over a medium heat, stirring regularly. Serve.

POTIMARRON SQUASH LASAGNE

Preparation: 15 minutes
Cooking: 20 minutes

118

serves 4

250 g (9 oz) celeriac (celery root), grated
4 sheets of Dauphiné ravioli, or lasagne
   (240 g/8½ oz)
500 ml (17 fl oz/2 cups) double (heavy) cream
salt and pepper
4 pinches of nutmeg

250 g (9 oz) potimarron (red kuri) squash,
   deseeded and grated
50 g (2 oz/½ cup) grated Emmental
150 ml (5 fl oz/scant ⅔ cup) water

26 cm (10 in) casserole dish (Dutch oven)

method

Make a layer of celeriac at the bottom of the casserole dish. Cover with a sheet of ravioli and spread 2 tablespoons of cream on top. Season with salt and pepper, add a pinch of nutmeg, cover with a layer of grated squash, then add another layer of ravioli. Continue to alternate these layers, until all the ingredients are used up. Top with a layer of grated cheese. Pour on the water, cover and cook for 20 minutes over a low heat. Serve.

RAVIOLI WITH SPINACH AND HAZELNUTS

Preparation: 5 minutes
Cooking: 3 minutes

serves 4

300 g (10½ oz) fresh ravioli
100 g (3½ oz) baby spinach
250 ml (8½ fl oz/1 cup) soya-based cream
1 tablespoon onion powder
2 tablespoons soy sauce

1 pinch of salt
1 pinch of pepper
50 g (2 oz/⅓ cup) hazelnuts, roughly chopped

30 cm (12 in) frying pan (skillet)

method

Put all the ingredients into the frying pan, setting aside half the hazelnuts.
Cook for 3 minutes over a medium heat, stirring to wilt the spinach.
Serve with the reserved hazelnuts.

RICE NOODLES WITH COCONUT AND LEEKS

Preparation: 10 minutes
Cooking: 10 minutes

serves 4

400 g (14 oz) rice noodles
4 small leeks, cut into strips lengthways
400 ml (13 fl oz) tin coconut milk
2 tablespoons soy sauce
400 ml (13 fl oz/generous 1½ cups) water

1 small bunch of parsley, snipped
50 g (2 oz/⅓ cup) peanuts, toasted, salted and
    roughly chopped, to serve

30 cm (12 in) casserole dish (Dutch oven)

method

Put all the ingredients into the casserole dish, setting aside half the parsley.
Cook for 10 minutes over a medium heat, stirring regularly. Serve with the
reserved parsley, snipped, and peanuts.

CANTONESE RICE

Preparation: 10 minutes
Cooking: 18 minutes

serves 4

250 g (9 oz/1¼ cups) basmati rice
1 carrot, finely diced
150 g (5 oz/1 cup) frozen peas
1 garlic clove, chopped
150 g (5 oz) smoked tofu
3 tablespoons sunflower oil

2 pinches of salt
2 pinches of pepper
500 ml (17 fl oz/2 cups) water

30 cm (12 in) frying pan

method

Put all the ingredients into the frying pan, except for the water. Sauté
for 3 minutes, stirring constantly. Add the water, cover and cook for
a further 15 minutes. Serve.

PAN-FRIED RICE WITH LEEK AND CELERIAC

Preparation: 10 minutes
Cooking: 20 minutes

serves 4

125 g (4 oz/⅔ cup) long-grain rice
2 large leeks, cut lengthways into narrow strips
350 g (12 oz) celeriac (celery root), grated
2 tablespoons coconut oil
370 ml (12½ fl oz/1½ cups) water
2 pinches of salt

2 pinches of pepper
2 tablespoons grated coconut, to serve
1 small bunch of parsley, snipped, to serve

30 cm (12 in) casserole dish (Dutch oven)

126

method

Sauté the rice, leeks and celeriac in the casserole dish with the coconut oil
for 5 minutes. Add the water, salt and pepper. Cover and simmer for
15 minutes. Serve with the grated coconut and parsley.

PAN-FRIED RICE WITH CARROT AND PEANUTS

Preparation: 10 minutes
Cooking: 25 minutes

serves 4

1 carrot, grated
1 parsnip, grated
250 g (9 oz/1¼ cups) basmati rice
2 shallots, finely chopped
2 garlic cloves, chopped
2 pinches of salt
3 tablespoons olive oil

1 small bunch of dill, snipped
50 g (2 oz/⅓ cup) peanuts, toasted, salted and
    roughly chopped
500 ml (17 fl oz/2 cups) water

30 cm (12 in) casserole dish (Dutch oven)

method

Sauté all the ingredients, except for half the dill, the peanuts and the water, in
the olive oil for 5 minutes. Pour in the water, cover and cook for 20 minutes.
Serve with the reserved dill and the peanuts.

RISOTTO PRIMAVERA

Preparation: 10 minutes
Cooking: 30 minutes

serves 4

20 g (¾ oz) butter
2 tablespoons olive oil
250 g (9 oz/generous 1 cup) arborio rice
2 shallots, finely chopped
250 ml (8½ fl oz/1 cup) white wine
1 vegetable stock cube
750 ml (25 fl oz/3 cups) water
2 pinches of salt
2 pinches of pepper
zest of 1 lemon

400 g (14 oz) green asparagus, cut into 2 cm
  (¾ in) segments
50 g (2 oz) rocket (arugula)
100 g (3½ oz/⅔ cup) frozen peas
50 g (2 oz/½ cup) grated Parmesan, plus extra
  to serve
4 sprigs of dill, snipped, to serve

30 cm (12 in) frying pan (skillet)

method

Melt the butter in the frying pan with the olive oil. Add the rice and shallots. Sauté for 3 minutes, stirring. Add the white wine and stock cube, then allow the wine to evaporate, stirring. Add the water, salt, pepper, half the lemon zest and asparagus. Cook for 20 minutes, stirring regularly. Add the rocket, peas and Parmesan. Cook for a further 5 minutes, stirring. Serve with the reserved lemon zest, grated Parmesan and dill.

VEGGIE JAMBALAYA

Preparation: 15 minutes
Cooking: 35 minutes

132

serves 6

2 tablespoons sunflower oil
250 g (9 oz/1¼ cups) long-grain rice
1 carrot, peeled and chopped
1 garlic clove, chopped
1 teaspoon paprika
1 pinch of ground cloves
1 pinch of chilli powder
1 teaspoon cumin seeds
1 tablespoon dried oregano
2 bay leaves
3 stalks of celery, finely sliced (set aside the leaves)

400 g (14 oz) tinned kidney beans, drained
1 tablespoon tomato purée (paste)
1 teaspoon salt
1 vegetable stock cube
4 spring onions (scallions), thinly sliced
500 ml (17 fl oz/2 cups) water

30 cm (12 in) casserole dish (Dutch oven)

method

Heat the oil in the casserole dish. Sauté all the ingredients, except the celery leaves, beans, tomato purée, salt, stock cube and 2 of the thinly sliced spring onions. Add the water, salt and the stock cube. Cook for 30 minutes over a low heat. Add the beans, celery leaves (snipped), tomato purée and reserved spring onions 5 minutes before the end of cooking. Serve.

RED RISOTTO

Preparation: 10 minutes
Cooking: 25 minutes

134

serves 4

20 g (¾ oz) butter
2 tablespoons olive oil
300 g (10½ oz/1½ cups) Camargue red rice
2 shallots, finely chopped
1 vegetable stock cube, crushed
1 small sprig of tarragon, snipped

2 pinches of salt
2 pinches of pepper
250 ml (8½ fl oz/1 cup) red wine
750 ml (25 fl oz/3 cups) water

30 cm (12 in) frying pan (skillet)

method

Melt the butter in the frying pan with the olive oil. Add the rice, shallots and stock cube. Sauté for 3 minutes, stirring. Add half the tarragon, the salt and pepper, red wine and water. Cover and cook for 20 minutes over a low heat. Serve with the reserved tarragon.

NERONE RISOTTO WITH RADICCHIO

Preparation: 10 minutes
Cooking: 1 hour

136

serves 4

250 g (9 oz/1¼ cups) Nerone black rice
1 radicchio (250 g/9 oz), finely sliced
1 shallot, finely chopped
6 tablespoons olive oil
2 tablespoons crema di balsamico (balsamic glaze)
2 pinches of salt

2 pinches of pepper
1.5 litres (51 fl oz/6 cups) water
150 g (5 oz) balls of mozzarella

30 cm (12 in) casserole dish (Dutch oven)

method

Put the rice, radicchio, shallot and olive oil into the casserole dish. Cook
for 5 minutes over a high heat, stirring continuously to wilt the radicchio.
Stir in the balsamic glaze, salt and pepper. Pour in the water and cook for
approximately 55 minutes, stirring regularly, until all the liquid has been
absorbed. Add the balls of mozzarella, stir and serve immediately.

WHEAT WITH PUMPKIN AND SAFFRON

Preparation: 10 minutes
Cooking: 25 minutes

138

serves 4

250 g (9 oz) pre-cooked wheat
800 g (1 lb 12 oz) pumpkin, peeled and cut into
    large chunks
1 pinch of saffron
250 ml (8½ fl oz/1 cup) soya-based cream
2 shallots, thinly sliced

500 ml (17 fl oz/2 cups) water
2 pinches of salt
2 pinches of pepper
1 small bunch of parsley

26 cm (10 in) casserole dish (Dutch oven)

method

Put all the ingredients into the casserole dish, setting aside half the parsley.
Cover and cook for 25 minutes over a medium heat. Serve with the
reserved parsley, snipped.

GNOCCHI WITH SPINACH AND SAGE

Preparation: 5 minutes
Cooking: 15 minutes

140

serves 4

20 g (¾ oz) butter
1 spring onion (scallion), finely chopped
3 sprigs of sage
500 g (1 lb 2 oz) gnocchi
300 ml (10 fl oz/1¼ cups) water
2 pinches of salt

250 g (9 oz) ricotta
150 g (5 oz) baby spinach
2 pinches of pepper
grated Parmesan, to serve

30 cm (12 in) casserole dish (Dutch oven)

method

Heat the butter in the casserole dish. Add the onion, sage and gnocchi.
Shallow fry for 5 minutes, stirring. Add the water and salt. Cook for
5 minutes. Add the ricotta, spinach and pepper. Cook for a further
5 minutes. Serve with grated Parmesan.

GNOCCHI WITH GOAT'S CHEESE, WALNUTS AND LEMON

Preparation: 5 minutes
Cooking: 10 minutes

142

serves 4

500 g (1 lb 2 oz) gnocchi
100 g (3½ oz/1 cup) walnuts
200 ml (7 fl oz/scant 1 cup) double (heavy) cream
3 spring onions (scallions), thinly sliced
1 teaspoon dried oregano
300 ml (10 fl oz/1¼ cups) water

2 pinches of salt
2 pinches of pepper
zest of 1 lemon
3 small goat's cheeses, such as Rocamadour, cut
   into pieces

30 cm (12 in) casserole dish (Dutch oven)

method

Put all the ingredients into the casserole dish, setting aside half the zest and 1 cheese. Cook for 10 minutes over a medium heat, stirring. Serve with the reserved lemon zest and remaining cheese.

ASPARAGUS GNOCCHI

Preparation: 5 minutes
Cooking: 10 minutes

144

serves 4

500 g (1 lb 2 oz) gnocchi
125 g (4 oz) mascarpone
400 g (14 oz) green asparagus, cut into 2 cm
  (¾ in) segments
50 g (2 oz/½ cup) grated Parmesan, plus extra to serve
1 spring onion (scallion), finely sliced

300 ml (10 fl oz/1¼ cups) water
2 pinches of salt
2 pinches of pepper

30 cm (12 in) frying pan (skillet)

method

Put all the ingredients into the frying pan. Cook for 10 minutes over
a medium heat, stirring. Serve with grated Parmesan.

GNOCCHI WITH COURGETTE AND HAZELNUTS

Preparation: 5 minutes
Cooking: 15 minutes

serves 4

500 g (1 lb 2 oz) gnocchi
250 ml (8½ fl oz/1 cup) milk, of any variety
2 courgettes (zucchini), grated
2 tablespoons miso
2 pinches of pepper
50 g (2 oz/⅓ cup) hazelnuts, chopped

26 cm (10 in) casserole dish (Dutch oven)

method

Put all the ingredients into the casserole dish, setting aside half the hazelnuts. Cook for 15 minutes over a medium heat, stirring regularly. Serve with the reserved chopped hazelnuts.

SOUPS

A range of simple, quick and comforting soups made all
in one pot. From traditional to fresh and contemporary,
the soups can be served in blended or chunky form.

BUTTERNUT SQUASH AND COCONUT SOUP

Preparation: 5 minutes
Cooking: 20 minutes

serves 6

1 kg (2 lb 4 oz) butternut squash,
   peeled, deseeded and cut into large chunks
1 onion, thinly sliced
400 ml (13 fl oz) tin coconut milk
½ stick of lemongrass, finely sliced
1 litre (34 fl oz/4 cups) water
2 pinches of salt
1 small sprig of coriander (cilantro)

20 cm (8 in) saucepan

method

Put all the ingredients into the saucepan, setting aside half the coriander.
Cook for approximately 20 minutes over a medium heat. Blend and serve
with the reserved fresh coriander, snipped.

CELERIAC SOUP

Preparation: 5 minutes
Cooking: 25 minutes

152

serves 6

500 g (1 lb 2 oz) celeriac (celery root), peeled and
   cut into large chunks
500 ml (17 fl oz/4 cups) water
500 ml (17 fl oz/4 cups) milk
1 onion, thinly sliced
1 vegetable stock cube

1 teaspoon salt
1 pinch of pepper
1 small bunch of parsley, destalked, plus extra
   to serve

26 cm (10 in) casserole dish (Dutch oven)

method

Put all the ingredients into the casserole dish and cook for approximately
25 minutes over a medium heat. Blend before serving sprinkled
with parsley, snipped.

CAULIFLOWER AND ALMOND SOUP

Preparation: 5 minutes
Cooking: 25 minutes

154

serves 6

500 g (1 lb 2 oz) cauliflower, cut into florets
400 ml (13 fl oz/generous 1½ cups) almond cream
600 ml (20 fl oz/2½ cups) water
1 onion, thinly sliced
1 teaspoon salt

1 pinch of pepper
1 tablespoon paprika, plus an extra pinch to serve
knob of butter, to serve

26 cm (10 in) casserole dish (Dutch oven)

method

Put all the ingredients into the casserole dish and cook for approximately
25 minutes over a medium heat. Blend. Serve with a knob of butter
and a pinch of paprika.

SWEETCORN AND PEPPER SOUP

Preparation: 10 minutes
Cooking: 20 minutes

156

serves 4

400 g (14 oz) tinned sweetcorn, drained
1 yellow (bell) pepper, thinly sliced
1 green (bell) pepper, thinly sliced
2 spring onions (scallions), quartered
1 pinch of hot chilli powder
2 tablespoons olive oil

1 vegetable stock cube
700 ml (24 fl oz/scant 3 cups) water
1 small sprig of coriander (cilantro)

20 cm (8 in) saucepan

157

method

Put all the ingredients into the saucepan, setting aside half the coriander. Cook for approximately 20 minutes over a medium heat. Blend before serving with the reserved coriander, snipped.

COURGETTE AND CHESTNUT SOUP

Preparation: 5 minutes
Cooking: 20 minutes

158

serves 6

750 g (1 lb 10 oz) courgettes (zucchini), cut into
  1 cm (½ in) rounds
300 g (10½ oz) preserved chestnuts
1 garlic clove
1 sprig of thyme, plus extra to serve
1 vegetable stock cube

250 ml (8½ fl oz/1 cup) almond cream
250 ml (8½ fl oz/1 cup) water
salt and pepper, to season

20 cm (8 in) saucepan

method

Put all the ingredients into the saucepan and cook for approximately 20 minutes over a medium heat. Blend before serving and season well. Serve with the reserved thyme.

SPINACH AND CHICKPEA SOUP

Preparation: 5 minutes
Cooking: 15 minutes

serves 6

500 g (1 lb 2 oz) spinach
400 g (14 oz) tinned chickpeas, drained
1 onion, thinly sliced
1 teaspoon cumin seeds
500 ml (17 fl oz/2 cups) soya-based plant drink
1 vegetable stock cube

250 ml (8½ fl oz/1 cup) water
1 pinch of salt
1 pinch of pepper

26 cm (10 in) casserole dish (Dutch oven)

method

Put all the ingredients into the casserole dish, cover and cook for approximately 15 minutes over a medium heat. Blend before serving.

LEEK AND GINGER SOUP

Preparation: 5 minutes
Cooking: 20 minutes

162

serves 4

250 g (9 oz) leeks, thinly sliced
100 g (3½ oz) potatoes, peeled and diced
100 g (3½ oz) silken tofu
10 g (½ oz) ginger, peeled and chopped
1 teaspoon curry powder

500 ml (17 fl oz/2 cups) water
2 pinches of salt
1 pinch of pepper

20 cm (8 in) saucepan

method

Put all the ingredients into the saucepan. Cook for 20 minutes over
a medium heat. Blend before serving.

PISTOU SOUP

Preparation: 10 minutes
Cooking: 20 minutes

164

serves 6

350 g (12 oz) runner beans, cut into 1 cm
  (½ in) segments
1 courgette (zucchini), diced
1 onion, chopped
2 garlic cloves, chopped
200 g (7 oz) tinned chopped tomatoes
400 g (14 oz) tinned haricot (navy) beans, drained
100 g (3½ oz) pasta shells
2 tablespoons olive oil

1 litre (34 fl oz/4 cups) water
2 pinches of salt
2 pinches of pepper
150 g (5 oz) pesto
2 sprigs of basil, to serve
grated Parmesan, to serve

26 cm (10 in) casserole dish (Dutch oven)

method

Put all the ingredients into the casserole dish, setting aside half the pesto.
Bring to the boil, then cover and cook for 20 minutes over a low heat.
Serve with the reserved pesto, basil (snipped) and grated Parmesan.

ASPARAGUS AND PEA BROTH

Preparation: 5 minutes
Cooking: 15 minutes

serves 4

400 g (14 oz) green asparagus, cut into
  2 cm (¾ in) segments
100 g (3½ oz/⅔ cup) frozen peas
100 g (3½ oz) small soup pasta
150 g (5 oz) small button mushrooms
1 vegetable stock cube

1.5 litres (51 fl oz/6 cups) water
2 pinches of salt
2 pinches of pepper
grated Parmesan, to serve

20 cm (8 in) saucepan

method

Put all the ingredients into the saucepan. Bring to the boil then cook for
10 minutes. Serve with the grated Parmesan.

VIETNAMESE SOUP

Preparation: 10 minutes
Cooking: 30 minutes

168

serves 4

150 g (5 oz/¾ cup) basmati rice
2 litres (70 fl oz/8 cups) water
1 small courgette (zucchini), diced
1 vegetable stock cube
40 g (1½ oz) ginger, peeled and grated

1 small sprig of coriander (cilantro), destalked
8 spring onions (scallions), snipped
1 lime, to serve

20 cm (8 in) saucepan

method

Put the rice, water, courgette, stock cube and ginger into the saucepan with half the coriander and 6 snipped spring onions. Cook for 30 minutes over a medium heat, stirring regularly. Serve with the reserved coriander leaves and spring onions, and add the juice and zest of the lime.

SPIRALISED BUTTERNUT BROTH

Preparation: 10 minutes
Cooking: 10 minutes

170

serves 4

400 g (14 oz) butternut squash, peeled, deseeded
   and spiralised or grated
1 leek, chopped
100 g (3½ oz) small soup pasta
200 ml (7 fl oz/scant 1 cup) single (light) cream
1 litre (34 fl oz/4 cups) water

1 vegetable stock cube
2 sprigs of rosemary
2 pinches of salt
2 pinches of pepper

26 cm (10 in) casserole dish (Dutch oven)

method

Put all the ingredients into the casserole dish, bring to the boil and cook for 6 minutes, stirring regularly. Remove the rosemary before serving.

UDON NOODLES WITH CABBAGE AND MISO

Preparation: 5 minutes
Cooking: 7 minutes
Resting: 5 minutes

serves 4

250 g (9 oz) Chinese cabbage, thinly sliced
150 g (5 oz) shiitake mushrooms, thinly sliced
1 piece of kombu
2 tablespoons miso
1.5 litre (51 fl oz/6 cups) water
1 teaspoon salt

400 g (14 oz) pre-cooked udon noodles
2 pinches of cayenne pepper, to serve
1 small bunch of chives, snipped, to serve

26 cm (10 in) casserole dish (Dutch oven)

method

Put all the ingredients into the casserole dish except for the noodles. Bring to the boil and cook for 5 minutes over a medium heat. Remove from the heat, add the noodles and leave to rest for 5 minutes, then stir gently to separate the noodles. Serve with cayenne pepper and chives.

SOBA NOODLES WITH TURNIP AND CARROT

Preparation: 5 minutes
Cooking: 10 minutes

174

serves 4

100 g (3½ oz) soba noodles
1 carrot, finely sliced lengthways
2 small turnips, grated (150 g/5 oz)
4 tablespoons soy sauce
1 tablespoon sesame oil
1.5 litres (51 fl oz/6 cups) water

2 pinches of salt
1 small sprig of coriander (cilantro)
1 tablespoon sesame seeds, to serve

30 cm (12 in) frying pan (skillet)

method

Put all the ingredients into the frying pan, setting aside half the coriander.
Bring to the boil then cook for 3 minutes. Skim. Serve with the reserved
coriander and a sprinkle of sesame seeds.

DESSERTS

Some intriguing dessert recipes with vegetables,
along with traditional dishes such as rice puddings –
each one perfect for rounding off a vegetarian meal.

MELTING CHOCOLATE DESSERT WITH COURGETTE

Preparation: 10 minutes
Cooking: 10 minutes
Resting: 20 minutes

178

serves 6

200 g (7 oz) dark cooking chocolate, chopped
3 eggs
80 g (3 oz/⅓ cup) sugar
50 g (2 oz/scant ½ cup) plain (all-purpose) flour
100 g (3½ oz) courgette (zucchini), grated

30 cm (12 in) frying pan (skillet)

179

method

Put all the ingredients into the frying pan. Cook over a very low heat,
stirring continuously with a spatula or a whisk, until the chocolate is melted.
Cover and cook for 6 minutes over a very low heat. Remove from the heat,
take off the lid, wipe away any condensation, then replace it. Leave to rest
for 20 minutes before serving.

BEETROOT PANCAKE

Preparation: 5 minutes
Cooking: 10 minutes
Resting: 5 minutes

serves 4

1 small raw beetroot (beet), peeled (100 g/3½ oz)
100 ml (3½ fl oz/scant ½ cup) milk, of any variety
100 ml (3½ fl oz/scant ½ cup) soya-based cream
2 tablespoons coconut oil
1 pinch of salt
50 g (2 oz/½ cup) walnuts

50 g (2 oz/¼ cup) sugar
100 g (3½ oz/scant 1 cup) plain (all-purpose) flour
1½ teaspoons baking powder
maple syrup, to serve (optional)

30 cm (12 in) non-stick frying pan (skillet)

method

Blend the beetroot with the milk, soya cream, 1 tablespoon of the coconut oil, the salt, 25 g (1 oz) walnuts and the sugar. Stir in the flour and baking powder. Heat the rest of the coconut oil in the frying pan. Pour the pancake batter into the pan and cook for 5 minutes over a low heat. Cover and leave to rest for 5 minutes. Slide the pancake onto a plate and turn it over. Return to the pan and cook for a further 5 minutes, then add the reserved walnuts. Serve with maple syrup, if liked.

BANANA AND BLUEBERRY PANCAKE

Preparation: 5 minutes
Cooking: 10 minutes

182

serves 4

1 banana
150 g (5 oz) silken tofu
100 ml (3½ fl oz/scant ½ cup) hazelnut milk
   (or other plant-based milk)
50 g (2 oz/¼ cup) sugar
2 tablespoons coconut oil

130 g (4½ oz/1 cup) spelt or wheat flour
1½ teaspoons baking powder
150 g (5 oz/1 cup) blueberries
maple syrup, to serve (optional)

30 cm (12 in) non-stick frying pan (skillet)

method

Blend the banana with the tofu, plant milk, sugar and half the coconut oil.
Combine the flour and baking powder and add to the mixture, stirring.
Heat the remaining coconut oil in the frying pan. Pour in the pancake batter,
press half the blueberries into the batter and cook for 5 minutes over a low
heat. Slide the pancake onto a plate and turn over into the frying pan.
Cook for a further 5 minutes and add the remaining blueberries before
serving with maple syrup, if liked.

COCONUT CHOCOLATE PUDDING

Preparation: 5 minutes
Cooking: 5 minutes
Resting: 2½ hours

184

serves 6

300 ml (10 fl oz/1¼ cups) full-cream milk
200 ml (7 fl oz/¾ cup) coconut milk
2 tablespoons sugar
1 teaspoon agar-agar
100 g (3½ oz) dark chocolate

20 cm (8 in) saucepan

185

method

Combine all the ingredients in the saucepan. Bring to the boil over a medium heat, mixing well and stirring until the chocolate is melted. Cook for a further 2 minutes, stirring continuously. Leave to cool untouched for 30 minutes, then refrigerate for 2 hours. Serve chilled.

VANILLA RICE PUDDING

Preparation: 5 minutes
Cooking: 40 minutes
Resting: 2 hours

serves 6

150 g (5 oz/generous ⅔ cup) short-grain rice
1 litre (34 fl oz/4 cups) full-cream milk
150 g (5 oz/generous ⅔ cup) sugar
zest of 1 lemon
1 vanilla pod (bean), split and scraped

26 cm (10 in) casserole dish (Dutch oven)

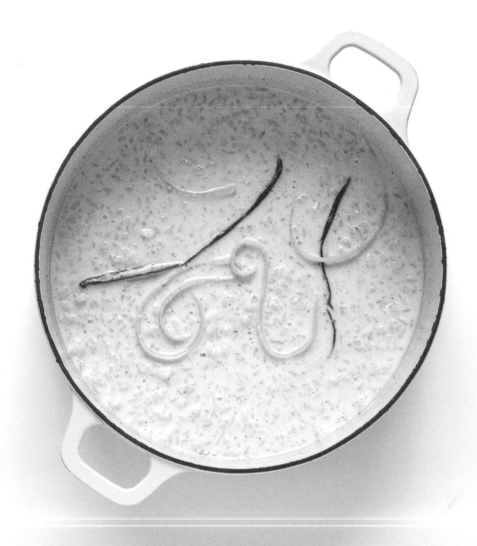

method

Combine all the ingredients in the casserole dish and bring to the boil.
Stir and lower the heat to minimum. Cover and cook for 40 minutes
with a wooden spoon placed between the pot and lid to prevent
the mixture from boiling over. Cover and leave to cool at room
temperature, then refrigerate for 2 hours. Serve chilled.

ALMOND RICE PUDDING

Preparation: 5 minutes
Cooking: 40 minutes
Resting: 2 hours

serves 6

120 g (4 oz/generous ½ cup) short-grain rice
1 litre (34 fl oz/4 cups) almond milk
150 g (5 oz/generous ⅔ cup) sugar
zest of 1 orange
flesh of 1 orange, sliced, to serve
30 g (1 oz/scant ¼ cup) almonds, chopped, to serve

20 cm (8 in) saucepan

method

Put the rice, almond milk, sugar and orange zest into the saucepan. Bring to
the boil, stir and lower the heat to minimum. Cover and cook for 40 minutes
with a wooden spoon placed between the pan and the lid to prevent the
mixture from boiling over. Cover and allow to cool at room temperature,
then refrigerate for 2 hours. Serve chilled with the orange slices
and the chopped almonds.

INDEX

First published by Hachette Livre (Marabout) in 2018
This English language edition published in 2019 by Hardie Grant Books, an imprint of Hardie Grant Publishing

Hardie Grant Books (London)
5th & 6th Floors, 52–54 Southwark Street
London SE1 1UN

Hardie Grant Books (Melbourne)
Building 1, 658 Church Street
Richmond, Victoria 3121

hardiegrantbooks.com

British Library Cataloguing-in-Publication Data. A catalogue record for this book is available from the British Library.

One Pot Vegetarian by Sabrina Fauda-Rôle
ISBN: 978-1-78488-257-0

For the French edition:
Proofreaders: Aurelie Legay and Véronique Dussidour
Typesetter: Chimène Denneulin
Photographer: Akiko Ida

For the English edition:
Publishing Director: Kate Pollard
Cover Design: Rebecca Fitzsimons
Junior Editor: Rebecca Fitzsimons
Editor: Kay Delves
Translator: Gilla Evans
Typesetter: David Meikle

Colour Reproduction by p2d
Printed and bound in China by Leo Paper Group

10 9 8